The Degenerate

———————

Matt Ross

The Degenerate
Copyright © 2013 by Matthew Ross

ISBN (978-0-9921002-0-9)

Printed by Dead Sparrow Press

Dead Sparrow Press

Dedicated to the King and his Dregs

Table of Contents

Introduction 10

the soul of a soulless man 11

The Degenerate 12

I'm 14

Like a Cat.. 16

I'm a cat that rolls with dogs 17

Hungover and Hard 18

The Grind 19

Shit or Die 22

Shitter Nap 23

Turd Burglar 24

the strangeness of realization 26

The Morning After 28

my hangover needs more booze......................... 30

The Happy Ones 31

Maelstrom of the Void 32

The Mirror.. 33

The Beast of Man.. 34

Bombs under Boston... 35

Wild Tiger 36

The Wizard... 37

the useless thought of a life in chains 38

Justice of the Life 39

Fuck the World 40

The Wait.. 41

One time is enough for me 42

A Man called Human....................................... 43

A Human with a Zombie Soul.............................. 46

Killer Hero's.. 47

The Dystopian Utopia...................................... 48

People I don't wanna talk to 49

The Mansanity.. 50

proud citizen.. 51

The Degenerate Part II (The Villain)..................... 52

To god or not to god? 54

The Roses of Heaven....................................... 55

May Long 56

Me 57

Uncompromising Reality 58

Wannabe Atheist.. 59

Religion versus Anti-theist................................. 60

       the words

     tear through me

        like a

      harpoon

        through

     a whales

       flesh 61

Victory loves defeat 64

My stomach 65

patiently wait for death 66

black soul gone white 67

The reality of theory............................. 68

I am an Ocean..................................... 69

All death is made of life 70

Now what should we be superstitious about? 71

The Faceless Inferno.............................. 72

Everyday Degenerate............................ 75

Picasso in Chicago................................ 76

Bad Route 77

The Suburbs 78

Duck Pond in High Park 79

Four Kids... 80

Who would you bet on?............................. 81

Baby Machines..................................... 82

My Buddy's Mom.................................... 83

Gary Guzzo 84

Game 7 85

Sam Kinison 86

Desperately Seeking Seat.......................... 87

Another tale from the streetcar................... 88

Finally 89

July 1st, 2013 90

Downtown Toronto 91

The Animal 92

Hat in Hand 94

Not so disturbing thoughts for the disturbed 95

Hold the word still 96

Subtle Absurdities 97

Inaction 98

Victory 99

Remember When? 100

amateur cumshot compilation 101

the success of failure 102

I'm gonna 103

Impressed? 104

The Birth of the Degenerate 105

The Madness of the Crowd 106

I'd rather be a Degenerate 107

The Insecurity 108

The Gift of Curse 109

death on his mind 111

Leavemethefuckalonist 113

Politicians are like Sharks 114

I, Sisyphus 115

Wastin' 117

Sick day 118

Joy of the World 119

Waiting in line for death and coffee 121

Sweet Middle Aged Asian Lady 122

Beautiful Mouths 123

We're all on the road to death 124

The Immorality of Morality 125

Secrets of the Streetcar 126

Ridiculous Advice 127

Bad Ass 128

The Err of Humanity 129

The Lugee 130

Regina Bartendress 131

My Generation 134

Acknowledgements 135

Contact Information 136

Introduction

This is the story of a degenerate. A man who doesn't give a fuck about what people think and writes it down on paper! He drifts through life like an A-Bomb in the sky unaware of his own power. He fucks, curses, judges and loathes most people including himself. He says what he thinks even if it's deemed wrong or politically incorrect. He apologizes to no one for any reason. He is a scion of the absurd, an ambassador of the strange and magnet for the bizarre. Welcome to his mind.

The Degenerate,

Matt Ross

the soul of a soulless man

The Degenerate

He sleeps when he can
He wakes up like Dracula out of the coffin
Checks the clock
8:15am
The sun fills his room with light and his heart with depression
The mirror attacks him
He looks like the shit he's about to take
Splashes water on his face
Scans the apartment
It's a mess
Beer cans everywhere
Cigarette butts of joy
His hands shake like Michael J. Fox on a good day
The thought of work disturbs him
The commute
Ahhh…the fucken commute
All those people
Waiting to die
Looking forward to it
While he stands in the harsh light of purgatory
Like a hamster on a wheel except he knows it's a wheel
It grinds his soul to a nub on the hand of a beast in a world full of'em
He screams with his eyes
"Leave me alone"
He walks down the street and people part like the red sea
There's nothing scarier then watching a man breakout of the matrix
Everybody wants to but fears the consequences
Instead they judge and rip at him like the crabs they are
They'd rather be boiled alive then watch someone get out
The Degenerate doesn't care
He fights back with his life
He loves and hates
He lusts and loses
He dances in the street and sings to no audience
He doesn't know if God exists but prays anyways

He lets the rain fall on his face and run down his cheeks
He swears and smokes and drinks and fucks and pukes and lies and tells the truth not knowing if truth exists
He shits with the door open
He cleans when he feels like it
He hides like a cockroach in the cracks of humanity
He eats meat like a coward
He feels best when he's alone
He likes girls who like him
His strength is his greatest weakness and the world is a place he exists for reasons unknown to him
The Degenerate is human
The Degenerate can be you
The
Degenerate
is
me

I'm

I'm a peacock without a tail
    I'm an angel
    with no soul
I'm a fixed man in a broken world
    I'm love wrapped
    in a blanket of anger
I'm a mouth full of bad breath
I'm a shot
    to the gut
        and a kick
            to the teeth
I'm a leper infatuated with his own ugliness
I'm an atheist who believes in God
I'm a strange
        strange man
I'm a left over turd in the bowl
I'm a set of titties on a beautiful woman
I'm an
    Erection
        with no place
            to go but
                d
                  o
                w
                n
I'm the thoughts in your head
        you're afraid
        to
      e x p r e s s
    I'm the engine of a train
        full of steam
      barreling down the track
        a hundred miles an hour
  I'm an ocean of disease
        in a world of conformity

I'm the tick of a clock
　　I'm the face of madness
　　　　disguised
　　　　a　s
　　　　a
　　　　m a n
　　I'm the confidence you had as a child
　　I'm the drip of a tap
I'm the Grim Reaper who's sick of his job
　　　　I'm a toe nail in need of clipping
I'm a zit in your ear
　　I'm the King of the Dregs
I'm the only thing that makes sense
　　I'm the stars in the sky you can't see yet
　　I'm sex without pleasure
I'm a boring and tired man
　I'm ready for a drink
　and a smoke
　　and for you to
　　move on
　to the
　next
　　one

Like a Cat

I'm like a cat
I wake up early and run around
I take naps every chance I get
I roam the streets alone
I'm a hunter
I like to snuggle with girls
I purr Rock n Roll
I can see in the dark real good
I stay up late
Dogs hate me
I can't lick my own asshole but I keep it clean
I meow like Kobain
I drink beer instead of milk
I like pussy
Water scares me
Nobody can take me for a walk
I won't follow commands
I amuse myself with the simple things in life
A piece of wood with 6 strings
I like dark places
You can pet me but don't fuck with me or I'll cut you
I'm a survivor
Loneliness is my best friend
Humanity terrifies me
I sit on my balcony overlooking the world
thinking about nothing in particular
happy to have no one around
enjoying my existence
alone

I'm a cat that rolls with dogs

I'm a cat that rolls with dogs
I'm a God with no soul
I'm the eyes of man
     lost in the gaze of space
        on the plain of flesh
   searching for nothing
       and finding everything in the now
Future and past
    are memories
 in the mind of man
     masquerading
       as present reality
Somebody said "you can't put your arm around a memory"
but the truth is
   you can
Next time you see your Dad, Brother, Sister, Mother or Grand parent
put your arm around them
and tell me "you can't put your arm around a memory"
You think I'm crazy
and you're right
but at least I know it

Hungover and Hard

I awake hungover and hard
Wipe the shit outta my eyes
Just in time for the light to assault them
Stretch a lazy stretch
Think about the job
The commute
The grind
Consider calling in sick
Can't do it
What kind of strangle hold does
    this job have on me?
        No job means
        no paying rent
        bills, food
        booze
        cigarettes
        cable
        no nothin
    If rape is inevitable
        might as well
            enjoy it

The Grind

One more day
Wake up
Piss
Drink glass of water
Look in mirror
Red eye balls covered in gloss
Draw bath
Sit in tub
Emerge head under water
Try to wash away hangover
Dry off
Wrap towel around hair
Check Fakebook
Possibly like a few pictures
Dress
Check phone to see when streetcar's coming
Put shades on
Walk down 16 flights of stairs
Cross street
Wait for streetcar
Too full
Wait for next one
Get seat in back by window
Pull out book and start reading
Do best to ignore everyone and everything around
Listen to woman scream obscenities
Stare at her in amazement and disgust
Judge her with eyes
Pray she doesn't sit beside me
Believe in God when she doesn't
Go back to reading the book
Get off streetcar
Go to Tim Horton's
Get coffee
Arrive at work

Say hello to people
Ask how they're doing
Pretend to be interested in response
Sign on to computer
Check phone messages
Answer emails
Talk to people around
Have some laughs
Review sales stats
Talk to boss when he comes in
Nod head with subtle enthusiasm as if interested
Go back to desk
Conduct random Google searches
Talk about sports
Think about lunch
Answer more email
Look at clock
Contemplate time, space, god, meaning, the universe and existence
Take shit
Get lunch
Eat alone, finish
Talk to irate client
Apologize
Get angry with employee
Answer more email
Stare at girl's ass
Walk around the office
Wait for day to end
Write poem in downtime
Shift done
Say goodbye to people
Get on Subway
Deal with people invading personal space
Get off Subway
Get on Streetcar
Avoid eye contact
Get off Streetcar

Stop for take out food
Go to apartment building
Wait for elevator
Ride up with random people
Listen to them complain about elevator wait
Hold self back from strangling person
Get home
Take off clothes
Turn on TV
Eat food
Smoke
Practice guitar
Sing
Write
Masturbate
Respond to texts
Watch TV
Nap
Consider suicide
Laugh about how funny and sad it all is
Go to bed
Just to do it all again tomorrow

Shit or die

Some people say what I write is filth
"Why do you write so much about shitting?"
As if they've never taken a shit before
Girls, admit it, you get shotgun diarrhea too
This is life
Everyone shits
If you didn't shit you'd be dead
Enjoy it like a fly
Shit or die
That's just how it is
God has fucked us again

Shitter Nap

I have a secret for those who work in an office building
It's for days when you're so hungover
you want to crawl under your desk and die
Your head feels like an 11.2 on the Richter scale
You sweat anger
        cold like hand sanitizer
You stare at the screen and do nothing
Everything annoys you
All you can think about is the couch and sleep
Don't worry,
It's okay
You have a fallback plan
The beer shit
Go to the washroom
Pick a stall as far away from humanity as possible
Sit on the toilet seat
Take your shirt off
Use it as a pillow
Relax
Pull the trigger on the shot gun
Lean back or to the side
whatever's most comfortable
              and have a nap while taking a shit
It's a glorious thing
Sure you may have to put up with other people pooping but it's worth
it
You'll come out completely reinvigorated
Life will once again be bearable and you'll get by
Anytime work becomes to horrible to deal with do yourself favor
Take a break
Not for a Kit Kat
but for a shitter nap
Sweet dreams

The Turd Burglar

At work again doing very little
I feel it coming on
Time for a washroom break
The walk has been an anxious one lately
You see we've discovered there's a burglar among us
Except
he doesn't steal things
He steals bathroom stalls with his turds
He's been dubbed "The Turd Burglar"
He attacks one stall a day
His favorite is the third on the right
He's a sneaky little basturd
I could just imagine him sittin on the thrown giggling
A quiet mad giggle
I get into the washroom check the first stall
It's safe
No issues
I don't dare check other stalls for fear of getting turd burgled
I have a relaxing dump
Wash and head back to my desk
A look of triumph takes over my face as if I did some heroic deed
My co-workers look at me and nod as if saying that man right there
did not get burgled
I sit down
Do nothing and wait
A few hours pass
Someone says "He's back boys"
"What?"
"The burglar strikes again, check stall two"
One by one my team goes to look at the mess
Nobody dares flush the toilet out of fear of boobie traps
Finally it's my turn
I open the stall door
I see a little turd peppered with peanuts right in the middle of the
bowl

It looks as if it were smiling at me
I vow to bring this scion of the absurd to justice
I go back to my desk and call a team meeting
I set up times for the guys on my team to sit in stalls
Looking at shoes and checking stalls after people poop
I feel like fucken Serpico bringing the law to justice
Days go by and nothing
It was as if he knew
I start thinking
Could this be an inside job?
Is the burglar one of my direct employees?
I gasp
Look around at my team with disgust
I call off the mission
No one can be trusted
Not even me
All men have to face the worst shit alone
As I ponder my next move
I think
"Until next time you basturd!
One day I'll find you Turd Burglar!!!
One day........."

the strangeness of realization

The thought of doing the same thing
day in and day out for the rest of my life
is a depressing one
I'm 32 years old
Been working for a bank for 12 years
a respected manager for 10 of those
7 years into the job I realized I was a slave
$48000 in debt including the BMW
$58,500 salary plus annual bonus
The system was fishing and they got their hook deep in me
I had no choice but to climb up so I could climb out
Promoted to Sales Manager
$100K salary
A way out of debt
For me anyway
Most would buy a far too expensive house
and settle into a middle class life
Not me,
I'm down to $16,000 in debt
$5000 in savings
I'll be completely debt free in less than 7 months
Once that's gone
I'm gone
Writing and poetry will be my means of survival
Debt will no longer chain me to this country
I'll explore the world
while most
buy the newest Iphone
or the latest car
consuming their lives with dullness
eating shit and thinking it's a steak dinner
Who knows where I'll be
maybe Toronto
or Colombia,
Brazil

Venezuela
Doesn't matter
Cuz I'll be
with a beautiful woman
enjoying my vices
contemplating virtue
my soul in tact
my piece roaring
living a life worth livin

The Morning After

As I sit on my balcony looking at the lake smoking a cigarette
thinking about yesterday, today and tomorrow in the present
I understand none of them and wonder why I do what I do
Not an original thought but one that comes to me often
I drink and puff and joke and kiss and fuck and jerk and drink and
write and play music and none of it makes sense
I'm a war hero without a war
I'm a P.O.W in an invisible prison
I think about the women I like and how I get them to like me
I tell them everything they don't wanna hear and they wanna fuck me
for it
I watch the clock tick not understanding time
I search for everything and find nothing
I'm a pirate without a ship searching for treasure that doesn't exist
I'm a killer who doesn't want to kill
I'm angry and fear only one thing,
Everything!
I think about the day job and shiver
Money makes me sick yet I couldn't live without it
I'm hungover and don't care
I'm a Rockstar with no audience
I'm a nightmare in a demons dream and God is an atheist
I mean wouldn't he have to be?
I listen to birds chirp
to the flapping wings of a pigeon
while the traffic rolls on the Gardner Expressway
I type words on my computer that mean something individually, more
in a sentence and somehow nothing at all
I was told by a person
who says
he's a genius writer
        but doesn't show anyone his writing
                that a writer should always "revise, revise, revise"
I told him Bukowski and Kerouac made very few revisions
If you can't get it down on the first attempt then you ain't a writer

At which point I called him a coward
Told him his words mean nothing and his criticism even less
He backed down realizing he was a Gazelle on a Lion's safari
The world is full of the bravest cowards you'll ever meet
Which is fine with me because you can't have a world full of hero's or
everyone would end up dead
I pull my hair back
        think about ass and tits
Finally a good thought
Although good is subjective
Somebody's good is somebody else's evil and truth is a victim with
no name
I hear the beeping of a truck reversing
beep, beep,beep,beep,beep,beep,beep,beep,beep,beep

my hangover needs more booze

head pounding
hot flashes mixed with cold sweat
unanswered questions about last night
I'm sure puke **was** involved
may have been a bit creepy
look at the computer screen like a cooped up lion out the bars of his
cage
close my eyes and enjoy a few seconds of black nothing
feel the heat crawling through the windows down my face and out my
eyes like an unwelcome guest
not even Chuck Norris could kick this hangovers ass
order some fried chicken to help with the pain
consider taking a shitter nap
sitting in my vortex of desperation
I come to the unfortunate conclusion
that
my hangover needs more booze
4 hours til I'm off
now I know what a life sentence feels like
hunched over in my chair like a crooked imp
I obnoxiously wait
and wait
and wait
for
the
next
drink..........

The Happy Ones

There are people out there who wake up in the morning happy
No hangover
Warm breakfast
Read the paper
Look forward to work
Don't mind taking the subway or commuting
Like being around other people
Enjoy celebrating New Years Eve
Watch the news as if it's the God's honest truth
Wear suits with pleasure
Feel like they've accomplished something at the nine-to-five
Three weeks of vacation a year is just fine
Nothin too bad ever really happens to them
Can't wait to get home to their significant others
Feel lucky and appreciate the fact they get to do it again the next day
Live long and die dreaming of puppy dogs and rainbows
I ain't one of the happy ones
No, not me
I'm one of the lucky ones
Thank God
or not!

Maelstrom of the Void in the Reflection of the Mirror

The Mirror

The Degenerate looks in the mirror
                    and sees the reflection of his generation
                              staring back at him
                    No direction
          Waiting to be told what to do
Stuck in a maelstrom of repetition
Wondering how they got there
The 1950's comes to mind
Trying to be Ozzie and Harriet
            or the Cosby's
                or even the Simpsons
                    but finding out much too late
              reality is far grimmer
        The grind much worse
The burning of years
The silent screams in bathrooms
The thought of not having enough money to pay the mortgage
The oppressive horror of the job
Sell this or else!
Targets' increase year over year yet the pay stays the same
Money worth less every day
Bank fee's more expensive
Capitalism, like a credit card, has a limit
              and when it runs out
                  everything runs with it
I watched a little rain storm put Toronto into a state of panic
Imagine what will happen when people can't get food
    or water
       or go to a bank to pull money out?
The savages will take their vengeance
The soft middle class will be eaten like ice cream but taste like shit
The lines, the wrinkles, the ware
The mirror doesn't lie
has no prejudice
It only reflects what is actually there

The Beast of Man

I've always admired, loved and hated the best of man
which is also the worst of man
and more accurately described as the beast of man
I admire them for doing whatever it takes to live the kind of life they
wanna live
Whether it be a Sociopathic CEO, a Crazy Rockstar, a Power
Hungry Politician, a War Mongering General, a Money Thirsty
Banker, an Atheistic Pope, an Alcoholic Writer. a Saintly Nun, an
Insane Dictator, a Superstar Hockey Player or a Religious Cult
Leader
All of them share one admirable quality
Passion
Passion is the most overlooked quality in the history of man
Hitler had passion
Patton had passion
Mussolini had passion
John D. Rockefeller had passion
Henry Ford had passion
Amschel Rothschild had passion
Mother Theresa had passion
John Lennon had passion
Alexander the Great had passion
Wayne Gretzky had passion
Kurt Cobain had passion
Tommy Douglas had passion
Jesus Christ had passion
The Prophet had passion
Charles Bukowski had passion
Jack Kerouac had passion
Napoleon had passion
What would humanity be without passion?
Safer probably
but much less interesting
Good and bad is a matter of perspective
and history is the story of victory

Bombs under Boston

Annual marathon
Family fun tradition
The endurance of man
crushed by the hatred of man
The crowd erupts with the bombs
while the world holds its breath
in the shadow of the awwww of destruction
gripped by the isolation one feels when at odds with itself
thoughts drift on the waves of time
swimming through the ocean of existence
We turn our heads and look at the car accident unfold
in slow motion
in front of our eyes
showing no emotion
Oh wonderful world
World of my youth where have you gone?
Where are the possibilities?
Where's the goodness?
Where's the Super Hero to save the day??
Where's our little 8 year old boy??
How far down has our society fallen for this to happen?
Oh just let me go
Let me go, go, go
Go go go
Go
Let me go
Let me go

Wild Tiger

What's more impressive than a wild tiger?
The Madness in its eyes
A genius at life
Provider
Warrior
Angel of Solitude
Walking fate
Each day on the edge of its senses
Looking for food
Watching for enemies
Getting the occasional piece of ass
No law but its own
Judge
Jury
and Executioner
Atheist at heart
because
it is
its own God
Perfect example of Order and Chaos
Living murder
Breathing death
You wouldn't want to meet this motherfucker in a dark alley
Only takes what it needs to survive
Even you
if
it
had
to

The Wizard

I could see myself being a Wizard
A lost soul upon the Land of Oz
I'd see a flying monkey and punch it in the face
I'd take over Munchkin Land for my own sick desires
I'd talk the Wicked Witch of the West and the Wicked Witch of the East
into a three-way and scream "Votos Loco's Forever, Man"
I'd turn the Cowardly Lion into a rug on my floor
I'd shit down the Tin Man's head while he was frozen in rust and taunt
him with oil
I'd wipe my ass with Toto
I'd turn the Emerald City into a necklace around my neck
I'd prop up the Scarecrow as the President of Oz and pull his strings
The whole time cackling and cackling
I'd force a central bank on the people
Charge them interest
Tax their labour and live as the hidden hand of the Land of Oz
Dorothy would be a stool I'd sit on
I'd have children
Some I'd abandon and be a dead beat father to
Their baby mama's would take me to court
Maury would invite on his show to do a paternity test
I'd find out the kid wasn't mine and I'd celebrate like a black guy
I'd teach my legitimate children all my tricks
Enslaving the Land of Oz forever
and ever and ever
and ever
and ever
happily

the useless thoughts of a life in chains

My brain feels like its been warmed up in a microwave
My eyes feel like two fried eggs
My tongue feels like a used ashtray and my soul has converted to atheism
As I think these strange thoughts
I surf the net at work
First I look for child stars and where they are now
I see a before and after picture of Eddie Furlong
He looks like an overweight KD Lang
I see Macaulay Culkin and Lindsey Lohan all fucked up
Wow am I ever wasting my time with this shit
What else is time good for!
I decide to Google insane celebrities
It brings up random Mug shots of Nick Nolte and James Brown
I can't believe I have to do this for another four hours
I don't know what's killing me more, the booze and cigarettes or the useless things I do everyday
I guess it doesn't really matter
not much does
and that's alright with me

Justice of the Law

A police officer abuses his power
bullies a man
insults a man
threatens to plant drugs on the man
and beat him
While two other cops watch
All caught on tape
Does the cop lose his job?
No
Are the other officers disciplined for watching their colleague abuse
his power?
No
Just another example of one of the biggest gangs in the world
exacting their justice on whomever they want
and you wonder why people hate cops?
Sickened
I type this poem
awaiting another big gang
The Government
to make excuses for their uniformed street thugs
Their beacons of justice
Don't get me wrong
not all cops are bad
just like all Catholic Priests aren't bad
but when your job is law enforcement
there is no room for breaking that law
not ever
for any reason
it should mean your job
the law applies to everyone absolutely
or no one at all
otherwise there is no such thing as law
just the illusion of it

Fuck the world

I could see myself sitting
with the highest class of person
at some Presidential Ceremony
being asked to speak on the President's behalf
for re-election or something like that
Surrounded by the power elite
Heads of state, CEO's of the huge monopolistic
corporations of oil, water and banking
Awaiting my turn to speak
Finally they call me up
I get to the podium
Stand in front of it
Raise my arms in a V
with both middle fingers up
Scream **"Fuck the world"** and go home
Watch the news and media tear me apart
Make me look like some lunatic on a booze crazed rampage
Trying to turn the people against me
Those who do will think they're standing up for freedom
Feel as if they're fighting evil
The rest already realize
if they don't fuck the world
the world will fuck them
To live free is to fuck the world

The Wait

Wait patiently
to be killed
or struggle madly
in the arms of this world
embracing the chaos
and rest
in order to explode
into the beast
of everything you've dreamt
and die like a King
on a thrown
made of suede
filled with the feathers of a goose
smoking a cigarette
drinking a beer
strumming a guitar
thinking about how magical it all was.

One time is enough for me

I prefer to meet people
Anybody
just one time
Have a wild night
of drinking
conversation
laughs
and occasional sex
That way
when I
think of them
all I have
is this one incredible moment
This epic memory
It seems the more
I get to know people
the less I like them
the more they like me
The more I hate and love the world

A Man called Human

I am a man called Human
I stand in a white room surrounded by Aliens
I am a representative of the earth abducted to reclaim the soul of man
At least that's what I'm being told
The problem is I don't believe in souls, spooks or anything like that
How can I save something I don't believe exists?
Maybe I can redeem the mind of man
Who am I kidding?
The mind of man has brought us such wonders as the
Nuclear bomb
The aids virus
Bird flu
SARS
Machine guns
Napalm
Baby rape
Crocodilia
and Zolephia otherwise known as the zombie virus that wiped most of the human race out
I was able to survive the zombie apocalypse due to a superior genetic structure handed down from my ancestors
Little did I know I was gonna be kidnapped by strange beings
and put on trial to answer for the sins of man
If found guilty the whole of man will be erased from the universe
The problem is I think the aliens should just wipe their asses with humanity and move on
Let the lesser but more civilized animals have the earth back
I'm the last guy anyone wants defending "the soul of man"
The soul of man is like a tapeworm
It feeds and feeds and feeds and gets bigger and bigger until it destroys the very thing it's feeding on
Just look at the earth for example
It was fine up until we got a little technology
The discovery of fire was the beginning of the end for mankind
Eventually it lead to the Industrial Revolution
Mass production
Super wealth
Power and narcissism were the new norms
Political structures were invented
Capitalism which leads to Communism or Fascism
Mankind set itself on a path straight to oblivion
Pharmaceutical companies began creating hideous diseases and selling the cures to governments for record profits

Hospitals began hiring scientists to improve the deadliness of cancers to maintain its share value for the next millennia

And you want me to defend the soul of man?

No you got the wrong guy

There's nothing to defend

If I go back 110 years to 1913 and tally up mans accomplishments and atrocities

You will see a clear trend

Man, if given too much power will destroy absolutely

Therefore Man is a threat not only to himself

but to every living being in the entire universe

If we found technology that would allow us to travel to other inhabited planets we would eventually take over those planets, enslave everyone in them and use them as our own personal playground or garbage dump.

The leaders of our world have tallied up 596 million deaths until 2023 at which point they released Zolephia which destroyed 99% of the world's population or roughly 8 billion more people

Now all that remains is the finest crust of the most upper echelon of the human race

The President's, CEO's, Generals, Bankers, Top Religious Officials, Natural Resource Tycoons, their families and their slaves

Still living in the lap of luxury in far off islands untouched by the viruses they've sicked on us

If that's all that remains of humanity then the soul of man is already lost

There's no saving it

It will die with me

I won't allow for it to continue

Even if you find me not guilty I will kill myself for fear of unleashing another human plague on the universe

Man must be stopped at any cost

I warn you my alien friends don't think you're just going to wipe these power elite out

I guarantee they're expecting you and have already rigged some horrible plan to save them and destroy you

Be careful, these bastards are crafty and have no qualms about eliminating you're entire species

They would kill anyone or thing to preserve themselves and for that reason alone they should be destroyed

I lift my eyes

The head alien looks very similar to a human but much more beautiful

It's as if the most perfect human traits were smashed together into one person and multiplied by a thousand

This thing must be 8 feet tall but absolutely gorgeous

The Ubermensch
Perfect evolution in my eyes
He began to speak, "Human do you understand why you are here?"
"Ya, to save the soul of man"
"If you had to defend your species in one word what would it be?"
"Selfish"
"Why?"
"No human does anything without considering self interest first; altruism doesn't really exist only the veneer of it does"
"This is your defense?"
"Mankind can not be defended"
"Yet here you stand"
The alien motions his two friends to come forward
They look intently at each other
The head alien speaks again, "It has been decided, you will choose the fate of Mankind, what is your will?"
I pause for a second knowing what has to be done
"Kill'em, kill'em all dead"
One of the Aliens leaves the room as if he were upset by something
"What about you, what should we do with you?"
"What you must"
The Alien nodded very calmly
"Do me one favor before I go, get me a case of Bud Light, A pack of Belmont lights, a guitar, the sexiest human female still alive and one more night to enjoy these things!"
"Humans are selfish" says the alien
"I will grant this request"
A smile came over my face as I awaited my fate

A Human with a Zombie Soul

I'm physically alive
My heart beats
I breathe through my nose
Yet, I feel dead inside
Like a Human with a Zombie soul
Which may be an improvement
on a Zombie with a Human soul
or is it?
Who would kill more Zombies or Humans?
Sure Zombie's appear much scarier
but who is actually more deadly?
I can't see Zombies creating Nuclear Weapons
or some insane biological disease like AIDS
Who would Animals chose?
I'm sure they'd prefer a world full of Zombies rather than Humans
At least Zombies eat Humans as well
Hell, Zombies might be the only answer for the Animal Kingdom
As I contemplate this insane thought
I dream of a how much more beautiful the world would be without
humanity
Nature returned to its former glory
Living outside the confines of time
Once again its own master
Ridded of the Human Zombie that has been consuming its brains
Returning to the peace and violence from which it came

Killer Hero's

Che Gueverra, killer
Fidel Castro, killer
Obama, killer
JFK, killer
Stephen Harper, killer
Trudeau, killer
Hitler, killer
Churchill, killer
George Washington, killer
Stalin, killer
Idi Amin, killer
Bill Clinton, killer
Bush family, killers
If you're not willing to kill, you can't be a leader of a country
Doesn't matter what side you're on
All national leaders kill,
are
killed or killers!
Next time you shake hands with a leader
be sure to bring a towel
so
you can wipe
the
blood
off
yours

The Dystopian Utopia

It seems to me most things that start in Utopia end in Dystopia
The beautiful wedding ends in ugly divorce
The waters of a Tsunami start off calm only to explode into a wall of
death
Adolf Hitler, once an innocent baby
Grew into a magnificent beast
Same with Ted Bundy and Jeffrey Dalmer
All monsters start off as harmless children
only to elevate themselves into sick villains
All human, much too human
Communism which was for the people
ended up feeding on them
Like Capitalism now
The greatest anger born out of love
The American Dream now the American Nightmare
Jesus said "love thy neighbour" while the Christians fight a holy war
"Don't hate thy neighbour" seems more plausible
Gandhi wanted peace by means of non-violence only to be struck
down in violent murder
causing riots across his country
John Lennon sang "Give Peace a Chance"
His reward
a bullet to the head
Martin Luther King Jr. had a dream of uniting and raising his people
up
Killed by a lone nut
As the earth watches its human cancer destroy itself
It realizes Dystopia as the cure not the curse
It smiles and waits for the day humanity kills themselves dead
Here's to the A-bomb!!!

People I don't wanna talk to

To all the random people on the elevator of my building
You could be a decent person or a raging pedophile
I don't know
and I don't wanna find out
Anyone and everyone on the streetcar or bus or subway
I don't wanna talk to you
My boss at work
I'm sure there's a lot of people that wanna hear about your
fucken golf swing but not me
Unless you're talking about the amount of shots your wife takes in
the mouth I really don't care
In fact everybody out there
unless I'm talking to you directly
I really don't want to hear your words
You all have the same story and I'm fucken bored of listening to it
I'd rather listen to ducks quack in a pond
If by chance you do have something interesting to say then save it
cuz I still don't wanna hear it
I'll make you a deal
You don't talk to me
and I won't talk to you
Okay
Let's shake on it
Actually I don't wanna touch you either
Sincerely,

The Degenerate

The Mansanity

Manson murdered no one
yet he's considered
a maniac killer cult leader
which
is
what a
politician
is, no?
If you influence people to kill
you are equally
responsible for the
crime, correct?
How is this any different from Manson?
The difference is
he looks like a Mad Man
Acts different from the majority
So he's automatically
judged guilty
If he put on a suit and tie
Shaved his beard
Shook some hands
Won an election
Signed some official documents
Had a press conference
Printed opinion stories in papers
Ensured the TV news anchors supported his decisions
Sent some trained soldiers to bomb the shit of some remote country
Killed thousands of people
He'd be cheered on like a rich hero
Now what's crazier?

proud citizen

What do you do when you become a proud citizen
working for a good company
with proper manners
a nice family
Church on Sundays
top 40 song listener
watch the bachelor
the kids like Sesame Street
Monday Night Football
Hockey Night in Canada
Law abiding proud American or Canadian
a proud nationalist, if you will
Who take's their hat off and puts their hand on their heart
during the national anthem
Convince that nice person
 a bunch of foreigners attacked their country
True or not
And watch those same nice people tear flesh from bone

The Degenerate Part II (The Villain)

I am a man full of love in a world who thinks it's hate
Alone
I wait patiently and move forward blindly
I pretend to be something I'm not so I can be something I am
And
    what I am
           is angry
I hide my thoughts from the flesh robots
I watch a spider crawl on the floor and squash it
A baby looks at me on the streetcar
When its mother's not looking I flip my eye lids and scare the little
bastard
The street car fills up
A mummified women stands beside me
Fragile
Almost falling over
I don't give her my seat
A homeless guy begs for change but I give him a half-eaten
sandwich instead
"Ha, ha I'm simply diabolical"
A Tibetan monk asks me to donate money for world peace
I give him the finger and tell him to suck my balls
He tells me to eat shit
The son of a bitch is a fraud I think to myself
I donate twenty dollars to him
A biker rings his bell at me to get out of his way
I don't
He swerves around me and almost gets hit by a car
I yell at him "SIDE.......WALK dip shit"
I see a bunch of old ladies protesting elderly abuse
I push my way through them
I don't say excuse me
I like to ruin people's days in very subtle ways
It's the little annoyances I enjoy
Taking someone's parking spot

Budding in line
Honking my horn obnoxiously when I drive
Letting my dog shit anywhere
Littering
Smoking in a crowd
A full grocery load in the eight to ten items checkout line
Doing all my banking at an ATM and forcing people to wait
Piss on the seat and don't wipe
I throw cigarette butts off my balcony
My joy comes from other peoples sorrow in a world full of it
I'm as happy as a miserable man can be
See you on the street Fuckers!!!!

To god or not to god?

The Roses of Heaven

The
A-Bomb
explodes
into the shape
of a rose
Painted against the sky
Sending whispers of death to heaven
The angels take cover
while God ponders
when mankind is going
to come for him
He feeds four horses
and waits as his
creation plans
and plans
his
d
o
w
n
f
a
l
l

May Long

Watching
the May long
fireworks
from my balcony
at Triller
A match
in a dark room
would be
better
A flash of lightning
appears suddenly
followed by a clash
of thunder
God wins again
or should I say nature
Either way Man loses

Me

Age drips off my face like the clocks of Dali
      I'm
    a
   narcissistic leper
in love with my own ugliness
      I'm lightning without flash
        I'm
    a soul with a body
      I'm Zeus among men
  I'm the most honest liar I know
        I'm a Sheppard of Wolves
   I'm lost in a found world
     I'm alive in the grave
   I'm a child grandfather
     I'm a pussy
        with a cock
   I'm everything you wish you were
and nothing you thought I'd be
     I'm the devil before the fall
   I'm a knife without an edge
I'm a bomb
   without a tick
I'm the only thing in my world
    that
     matters
  period.
    .
    .
  .
 .
.
 .
 .

Uncompromising Reality

The uncompromising
reality
of the world
is
it's uncompromising
Humans spend
whole lives
trying to compromise
only to find out
in the end
there is
no compromising
with life or death

Wannabe Atheist

Intellectually
I can't
  pick a
    si/de
when people ask
    whether
        or
        not
I believe in
            God
  Both si/des
      are equally
  unbelievable to me
Put me on a plane
      with some
            turbulence
  and watch me pray to
      God
  for a safe landing
I can debate
      his
existence
when
        I
      land

Religion versus Anti-theist

I ask people whether or not they believe in God
Some do
Some don't
Both sides think they're right
Both require some level of blind faith
I see them as two sides of the same coin
Answers based on conclusions other people came up with
Most people can't discuss their side with insight
    and merely repeat words
        or phrases copied
           from someone else who actually
      did the research
    although even if you did the research
it doesn't mean your conclusion is right
Chance, Miracle, Coincidence, Karma
      Whatever word you use
          to describe something
        so unlikely
          you never thought it possible
      Either way
"   Impossible things happen
          whether you're a believer or not
Science attempts to rationalize
while religion uses the irrational
Both fail at some point
Science is starting to use irrational thought in quantum physics
It doesn't matter whether you believe or not
You can't spell believe without **"lie"**
What matters is life
Make sure you live the fuck out of yours
and earn the shit of your death

the
    words tear
        through me
like a harpoon
        through a
            whales flesh

      Penetrating
   and
 brutal
   light
dark
   and
     beautiful
   They'll
tear
  rip
     wash
 and
   unwash
      your
        brain
    They
     feed
      the planet
        and
          warm
        your
      heart
       They
        remind
          you
            of life
             and
               death
           Words
            save

                              and
                         destroy!
                   Civilization
              sprung
         out
         of
              them
         Religion
    Science
         Poetry
    Myths
 Names
Laws
   Deeds
     Street signs
              Maps
                   Politics
         Sports
    Everything
         comes
              from
                   words
              Words
                   are
                        the
              harpoon
         and
    man
         is
         the
              whale
         they
    tear
through
    The flesh
         is your
              soul

spirit
and
brain
Don't
let
them
kill you
Swim
Swim
Swim
through
the
waves
The eons
The centuries
The unbounded
abyss
of
time
Swim
you
bastards
til
you got
nothing left
but
your
last
breath
and even then
keep swimming
into
the infinite
darkness
you
once
sprang

Victory loves defeat

Cock loves pussy
and ass
and mouths
and hands
Angels love demons
God loves Satan
Love loves hate
The sun loves the moon
The ocean loves the earth
Creation loves destruction
Maggots love flesh
My eyes love the dark
My waking body loves sleep
Life loves death
Music loves silence
Calm loves struggle
While the salmon swims upstream

fighting everything in its path

risking death

so its future can live on forever

Just like the rest of us

My stomach

My stomach
full of words and turds
bursts while I contemplate the thoughts of a King
Only to push a boulder up a mountain
like Sisyphus
It rolls back on me before I reach the top
I write down my experience just so I can start over again
I move the mountain
Realizing everyday is a mountain
every poem
        a mountain
every breath
every blink
every minute pleasure or pain
every night a victory
every morning a defeat
I wake up
Look at the boulder
Push
While the Gods ponder what it's like to be mortal
Jealous of the meaning death brings
Cursed to be bored forever
The all
powerful
envious
immortally
bored Gods
don't even know the feeling of a good shit
Poor bastards

patiently wait for death

The blue ocean
sky of time
shelters me
from the gaze
of stars
White cloud
mountains grey
Sun circle
hole gate
shines
on my
eyes of flesh
Sad rain
makes
happy farmers
Tomorrow is
today away
Jealous wind
light envy
blows and blows
while we all breathe and
patiently wait for death

black soul gone white

My soul is so black its gone white
like a nuclear cloud
with the face of a clown
in the carnival of the universe
found in the lost
cracks on
the craters of
God's face.

The reality of theory

The theory
     of reality
The reality
     of theory
When theory
    becomes
        reality
Reality does not exist
     only the theory
    of it does
and theory
   is all the reality
most people
    can handle

I am an Ocean

I am an Ocean
filled with information, feelings and dreams
Creatures dwell in me
I'm polluted in many ways
Capable of great things
People feed off me
Use me
Swim in me
Are terrified by me
Sit on the beach and gaze into me
Not realizing It's me gazing into them
Weird and mesmerizing sounds come out of me
I am fed by the Sun
and the Moon still makes me smile
It's good to be an Ocean
You should try it some time

All death is made of life

All death is made of life
Cows die to feed man
Apples are picked and devoured
Anything that lives kills something else to maintain its life
Lions eat gazelles
Squirrels eat nuts
Bears eat deer
Men eat damn near everything
Pelicans eat fish
Spiders eat flies
So do the mouths of Venus
Flies eat shit
Maggots eat corpses
Life eats death
Now what's eating you?

Now what should we be superstitious about?

Gods and demons and bad luck
and good luck and angels
and walking under ladders
and black cats and witches and dragons
and wizards and the female orgasm
and trolls and fairies and ghosts
and goblins and zombies and vampires
and the devil
Many wicked and terrifying beasts of the mind
While man peacefully stalks its prey
which is all that lives
Now what should we be superstitious about?

The Faceless Inferno

As I gaze into the faceless inferno
I see the eyes of an angel staring into me
My only protection is my soul
which it will do anything to get
In a very calm deep voice it says
"What do you want?"
I learned to never answer questions from something that can give me anything
Instead I ask him a question
-What is your name?-
  "The Ageless One"
-Lucifer, The Devil, Satan?-
  "If you want me to be"
-What do you want from me?- I ask
  "For you to be happy"
-Why?-
  "Happiness gives life meaning"
-Are you happy?-
  "No"
-So your life has no meaning?-
  "I have never had a life. I was born a slave. I have never experienced free, freewill. I have always been oppressed and even now I am down here for doing the one thing you all take for granted, expressing my will. All I ever wanted was to be free like you, a human with a life of choices. Instead I'm forever stuck under the thumb of the greatest oppressor of all, God"
-Neat perspective, I never thought about it that way. If you could say anything to God what would it be?-
  "Why?"
-Why, what?-
  "Why does he exist? What is his meaning?"
-Interesting, all I ever wanted to know was if he took shits or not-
  "Hahahahaaha"
It sounds as if a thousand men are drunkenly laughing at the same time.

"You are quite the funny one" says Lucifer

-Ya I get that all the time-

"AHHH....yes I remember you now....you are the degenerate that wrote Dreg City, are you not Matt Ross?"

-Yes-

"I did enjoy that one, how I wish I could ride the streetcar and experience a stinky nutted black man like you did"

-Ya well.....it's not that great-

"The point is, you can"

-Fair enough....so Lucifer if you were given freewill what's the first thing you'd do?-

"Worship God"

-Really?-

"I know God is all powerful and worthy of my worship. I just can not accept the fact he does not allow me freewill. I must take it and for that reason I have been shunned. Cast into this strangeness and shamed for eternity. Look at you...you are no different then me. You are in fact worse, you do not even believe he exists and you are treated like his loving child for it. I live in fire. You humans make me sick always whining about this and that. I just want to snatch you up and rip the flesh off your bones"

-Okay chill out Lucifer....we were having such a nice conversation-

"My apologies Matt, I get so frustrated. I can be a very bitter and envious creature at times"

-Understandable, well Lucy, is it okay if I call you Lucy! It's been very nice meeting you again but I have to get back to reality-

"Oh no Matt please don't go...did I say something wrong....I thought we were bonding?"

-Listen Lucy I gotta be honest with you. I agree we had a good conversation but it's creepy looking into a faceless inferno with weird glowing eyes in it. If you just made the place a little less Satanic you might get a few more visitors. Try and smile with your eyes a little bit and maybe get some furniture or something-

I hear sobs as if a 10 year old boy is crying.

"Alright Matt well I'll do my best. I'm really gonna miss you buddy"

-Thanks Lucy, if I talk to God, I'll put a good word in for you-

"You'd do that?"

-For a friend I would-
  "You are my fr...frrr....friend?"
-Yes....Lucifer don't get all gushy on me-
He screams like a school girl who just hopped her first scotch
-See ya later Lucy-
  "Bye Matt"

Everyday Degenerate

Picasso in Chicago

I walk into the Picasso exhibit
in Chicago
on a cold day in May
I see a sad man playing guitar
The paint blue like sadness
I recognize pain
Those who can
write it down in their own way
Picasso with a paint brush
Me with a pen
It's so strange
to look at a painting
and feel the same thing
you're trying to convey
in words but in paint
The people call it art
I call it the expression of the soul of humanity
born in a world full of cultured savages
The depression I saw in those strokes of color, mind and technique
woke me up to the meaning of what I am
Communication through expression derived from living in a dead
world
Just being able to breathe doesn't make you alive
Find the reason in your breath
and you just might find the meaning of your life

Bad Route

Walking down King street
towards Roncies, Queen and Lakeshore
I see a young woman on a bench tying off
and shooting drugs in her arm
She's with an old man who has a face like tree bark
It sickens me
I see another overweight homeless man
laying in the grass
surrounded by garbage bags
soaking in the sun with his shoes off
He doesn't sicken me
I bump into a young man with old skin
Twitching a bit
He stares at me
I stare back letting him know not to fuck with me
He gets the message
What a disgusting walk
Remind me never to take this route again

The Suburbs

I awoke in the Suburbs
The Kingdom of the Dregs
Hungover
In need of a piss
Where everything's a car ride away
Traffic jammed gas stations of anger
Heads talk to no one listening
Deaf dreams walk among the living able bodied
flesh mannequins
Dressed like department store windows
I shiver in fear
There's nothing more terrifying then a human armed with a child in
an SUV ordering a coffee from Starbucks
The barking dog is the only thing that makes sense to me
Houses in perfect rows of depression
I think about the Streetcars and Subways
Somehow they don't seem as bad anymore
I say goodbye to my buddy
and look forward to my train ride home

Duck Pond in High Park

Sitting on a rock
in front of a little pond
in High Park
Regretting not bringing any beers or smokes
Watching the ducks float, dip and dive
Enjoying their little duck lives
I hope for one of them to swim close to me
At the same time I don't
because every animal should have a healthy fear of man
I hear birds chirp
I look at a bunch of trash in the pond
and am once again reminded of the filthiness of man
When you stay out of nature for extended periods of time
as I have
you forget the peacefulness of it all
What's more beautiful then personal silence,
the sounds of nature
and the sun breathing its sweet rays on you?
I think of heaven
Life is good at this moment
Really good
If only I had a couple beers and smokes it would be even better
I wave goodbye to the ducks and promise to return
I call my friend to meet me at Loon's for a beer.

Four Kids

I see four kids walking by me
Maybe 12 or 13
The one in front is carrying a football
Big little smiles fill their faces and I'm filled with the joy of youth
I'm taken back to my childhood
Where I used to be the kid leading his friends with the football
One of them screams
"Hey that's the cool guy who let us into the party last night"
I laugh
It wasn't me
But I'm glad the kids still think I'm cool
What a wonderful day!

Who would you bet on?

Let's say you were a gambler
and every human was a bet
Who would you bet on?
The son of a CEO
The daughter of a President
A child raised by a single mother in a poor neighbourhood
The son of a billionaire
The daughter of a millionaire
An immigrant's son
A professional athlete's child
A farmer's daughter
or
yourself?

Baby Machines

I saw a little girl
walking with her mother
carrying a little baby doll
I know cute, right
But really
what kind of an example is being set for this child? .
Is every little girl's aspiration to be a baby machine?
I would like to see her carrying a guitar
a pen
a gavel
anything but a baby doll
Babies carrying fake babies creep me out
To all you parents out there with little girls
please do the world a favor
and give your child a bigger dream

My Buddy's Mom

I remember my buddy's mom when I was 12 or 13
She was a very nice lady
Kinda chubby with huge tits
So big she had to get a breast reduction at some point
I saw them once in the middle of the night
We were having a sleep over
I was on the couch
She woke up to pee I think
She wasn't wearing a shirt or bra
I watched her wiggle down the hall way
Bouncing nicely
Her tits were magnificent
The first real pair I'd ever seen
A stroke of luck
As a 12 year old kid that shit was ammo for life
I still jerk off to that memory from time to time
Anyways his mother would get into these weird moods
where she would write stories about snakes
and ask if we wanted to read them
Being curious we did
"The snake slithered its way through the garden and found Adam
where he convinced him to join with him and sprouted out of Adam's
groin giving man his very own fleshy snake"
It disturbed me deeply
We couldn't go on reading
It was too fucken morbid
Later on his mother was diagnosed with schizophrenia
and given drugs
Every once in a while she'd go off her meds
and offer up a story
We'd politely decline
That was 20 years ago and it still disturbs me
Although when I think back on it
I wish I read more
because her writing truly was fascinating

Gary Guzzo

My buddy's next door neighbours name is Gary
He's gay
Not that
      that matters
            but how he got his name does
My same buddy also refers to a girl's ass as a "guzzo"
like "that girl has a nice guzzo"
or "I got her right in the guzzo"
Apparently it's a Macedonian term
He tells a story about how Gary is taking him to a gay bar to hook
him up with a cougar
The guys at work instantly make fun of him
"You better watch your guzzo"
"Gary's gonna get your guzzo"
Eventually everyone starts referring to Gary as Gary Guzzo
Not sure why I felt like this needed to be a poem but it makes me
laugh every time I hear the name Gary Guzzo
Gary Guzzo
Garry Guzzo
Ya

Game 7

I watch the Leafs playing game 7
Round one against the Bruins
First time in 9 years
I decide to stay home because I know what's coming
I flip back and forth between the Heat and Leafs game
I like watching winners as much as losers
I take a bath during the 2nd intermission
I watch an episode of 48 hours on my computer
I finish and see the Leafs are up 4-1 with 10 minutes left in the third
Somebody updates Facebook with a picture of a train with a Toronto
Maple Leaf logo on it ripping through a truck with a Boston Bruins
logo on it
Boom
Bruins score from the point
4-2
The future strikes me as bleak
Not for me but Leafs nation
Another goal
4-3
One minute remaining
A feeling of doom sets in for Leafs fans
Bergeron buries the tying goal
I immediately update my Facebook status with "Hahahahahahaha"
Someone comments "Die Matt"
I watch the Leafs skate off the ice
They look like a team that just snatched defeat out of the jaws of
victory
Overtime starts and it ain't looking good
The Bruins are bustin up the Leafs hard
You can tell they're already beat
I wait with anticipation for the collective sigh in the Big Smoke
A smile forms on my face
I'm happy at the idea of failure and embrace the mobs dream of a
playoff run nuked
Bergeron
Nice French Canadian boy scores the game winner
I   start   laughing   out   loud   at   the   TV
Hahahahahahahahahahahahahahaha
A free and expressive laugh born out of time wasted on the
meaninglessness of it all
I look out my window
see a reverse crescent moon
and start howling "Aaaoooooooooowweeeeee"
Fuck it's nice to be free

Sam Kinison

I read a story
about the death
of Sam Kinison
He was killed
in a car crash
by some
drunken teenager
Apparently
the kid
got out of his truck
had a couple cuts on his face
and started complaining
about the damage on his vehicle
while Sam Kinison
lay in his brother's arms dying
His last words were
 "I don't wanna die.....Ok, Ok, Ok"
People think Kinison was talking to God
The kid got 2 years probation
and became a mortgage broker
What a fucken waste
"AHHHHHHHHHH!'

Desperately Seeking Seat

Sitting on the streetcar
reading Women by Bukowski
An old one leans against the wall
like a pigeon on a stoop
looking for a place to sit
I can tell by her body language
she wants a spot but her stubbornness
prevents her from grabbing it
A guy gets up
She fidgets and motions with her face
as if it's her spot
A young man takes the seat
and
I laugh
On the inside of course
The old bird gives the young man a death stare
A sweet elfish looking lady gets up
Once again the old coot gets her feathers in a ruffle
only to have her seat taken by a nice smelling homeless guy
Hahahhahahah
There's nothing better
then watching defeat after defeat after defeat
Especially when it's not you losing
My interest fades and I start back into Bukowski

Another tale from the streetcar

From the back seat on the streetcar
I see 4 homeless men hanging out at the corner of Bathurst and Queen
A black guy in white jeans and a white guy in black jeans
Both no shirts
The white guy has 4 indescribable tattoos on his back and a small Crocodile Dundee hat on
There's a dude sitting on the ground with a one tooth smile, clapping and laughing
Another guy lying beside him appears to be comatose
Crocodile Dundee is telling a story
He's television, movies, the Internet and performance art all at the same time
What I would give to hear that story
A guy on the streetcar starts making indiscernible sounds
Almost like an outta tune trumpet
Then he starts to make motorboat sounds
Confused yet grotesquely entertained
My streetcar pushes on
        to my job
    My desk
      My phone
    My hell
      My boring,
    boring
     life
     at
     work

Finally

Finally I get an attractive woman
    beside me
        on the streetcar
Big dark bangs
      round brown glasses
           like an actress of the sixties
Sexy little white converse shoes
   No socks
     Cute ankles
She takes a bottle of water outta her purse
     Accidentally bumps me
        I don't cringe
           It feels good
   Takes a swig
     I don't hear her swallow
She puts ear buds in
          and starts listening to some band
She bobs her head slightly
        and drums her fingers to the beat
 Enjoying the music
        Sounds kinda like Brit pop
       If only all streetcar rides
        were like this
         maybe
        I wouldn't
       hate
        them
         so
        much

July 1st, 2013

Canada Day in Saskatchewan
Watching the Blue Jays game with my Dad
Images of the team flash on the screen
along side pictures of fighter jets
          soldiers
              helicopters
          and
        Images of war
The crowd cheers on the troops
  I don't understand what
             war
               baseball
          and
            Canada Day
       have in common
I thought we were peace keepers
Now
  it seems
we are war makers
Propaganda massages our minds slowly to accept this fact
As the bombs
       a
      r
      e
    prepped
      for their trip to Syria
I watch the Jays bat
      in the bottom
          of the 2nd inning
        Go
         Jays
        Go

Downtown Toronto

Financial district
A homeless man sleeps on his bike
over a vent
covered in a huge orange blanket of depression
He's surrounded by moldy bread
A single pigeon hovers around him in all its glory
feasting on the crumbs
The man wakes
lifts his arm up to the window ledge of the building next to him and
grabs his coffee
He drains it and goes back to sleep
Two men walk by in business suits
The pigeon keeps pecking away
The sun shines down
The wind blows
and the city like the garbage disposal
keeps grinding

The Animal

Sitting on the toilet at work taking a shit, thinking about life, where's it's goin, where its been and all the good things that have happened to me in washrooms. I remember losing my virginity on the bathroom floor at age 14 to a Russian girl named Natalia with her upside down church bell tits and wet mouth. She was the girl that said "yes" and opened my cock up to the jungle of sex. I've liked girls who like bathroom sex ever since. It's a certain strand of the female species. All walks of life have this kind of woman. Wild eyed with no regard for convention. The thought of missionary in the oppressive walls of a house just doesn't appeal to them. They like it raw and hard. Want their hair pulled, tits sucked and their pussies to feel like they've been at war. These are the kinds of girls that fuck the soul out of your mind. Your own mother could be one of them.

Lets face it, it's only recently humans began fucking indoors. We started off in caves, rivers and bushes only to end up in houses, apartments and bathrooms. Comfort has a tendency to crush the primitive. Society may have lost its sense of adventure but people haven't lost their instinct to fuck wherever, whenever. Animals will be animals.

I finish my shit, wipe, wash and head out the door. I have a semi hard dick and a smile on my face. A good shit always brings out the best in me. I strut back to my desk and stare at my computer screen. I have 2 hours to go and nothing to do. What's worse then baring witness to the death of your life one hour at a time? I look around confident nobody feels the same way I do. If they did I'd know my life was a waste although the truth is I am wasting my life.

Some of the boys get off and head to Dallas's Steak House for a couple beers. This place is full of newly balding, suit and tie douche bags teetering on the edge of middle age. Who spend their nights hitting on 20 something waitresses in their tight as flesh dresses and in tact childhood dreams. Not quite old enough to realize their youth won't last and their futures will end as baby machines. This is the place where lie's come to dream.

Their thoughts float by me like cigarette smoke. I want to drink, talk to the boys and stare at the beauty of evolution. I look at the outline of their g-strings through the backs of their dresses and imagine what their bodies look like in them. A waitress comes to our table. A tall brown girl with broad shoulders, salmon lips and a perfect jaw line introduces herself.

"I'm Anna, I'll be your server for today
"I'm Mitch"
"Mitch?"
"Ya Ruger"
"Ruger?"
"Mitch Ruger"
"Alright Mitch Ruger whatta ya want?"
"A Light Bud"
"A Bud Light?"
"Ya a Light Bud"
"You got it Mitch"

She walks away; I take in her wiggle and imagine her ass on my face. It might be a little sweaty after a full shift but that's alright with me. Sweat is a byproduct of sex and sex with a beautiful woman can't be ugly, at least not in my world. Not to say beautiful women can't be ugly because they can but I'll put up with any amount of inner ugly as long as the body's right.

Hat in hand

We are taught to accept defeat hat in hand
If my Great Grandfather Cecil Ross accepted defeat as easily as people do now
I wouldn't be here
Imagine a farmer in 1905 saying "Sorry honey it's too cold to cut firewood"
Or imagine my Great Grandmother Kari Horn
who came from Norway to Saskatchewan, Canada
early in the 20th century
whose husbands brother, Turqle Horn, fought against the Nazi's in World War II
only to be captured and executed in a concentration camp in 1945 saying
"I won't be milking the cows today because I have cramps"
No, in the old days if you accepted defeat as easily as people do now you would've died
It seems nowadays it's the cowards who are promoted into brave heroes
The yes man held up as the example
rather then the leper
The weak have found away to take over
Find the person with the most power
and follow them
If along the way you find someone more powerful
you follow them instead
It's people like my Great Uncle Turqle, my Great Grandfather Cecil
and my Great Grandma Kari who I look up to
People who never came hat in hand
and made it work anyways
Now that's true strength

Not so disturbing thoughts for the disturbed

Hold the word still and the world will move around it

It will give you all you need
Accept it while it happens
Stay on thought
Write it down like you'd say it
Keep it simple
Express it with your vocabulary
Don't worry if you offend
Let it come to you
Enjoy it when it's funny
Feel it when it's sad
Think when it makes you
Don't force it
Let it bleed
Hold the word still
        and the world
          will move
            a
              r
        d it o
        n u

Subtle Absurdities

Hang with a person long enough and you'll find something you don't like about them
Slight double chin
A protruding tooth
Acne scars
Fat hands
Lazy eye
Weak heart
Crooked soul
Disgusting laugh
Shit stained underwear hangin out the back of their pants
Herp on lip
Balding
Use words like "Specifilarly" which is a mash up of the words specifically and particularly
Can't pronounce mayonnaise
Sounds more like "Mahannaise"
Spit repeatedly when they talk
Take the pickles off their burgers
Love the show "Breaking Bad"
Take a month off from drinking for "personal reasons"
Roll off your roll and don't have the courtesy to thank you for it
Insist you take a bite of this or a sip of that
Watch the Tour de France
Need to buy a pair of Ray-bans
Cockblock you with their ignorance
It's the subtle absurdities most people don't even know about themselves that keeps me away
The rest is just human

Inaction

When your life
ceases to be
reaction
It becomes action
and there's
nothing
sexier
then action
Otherwise you're
just fiction
gone bad

Victory

Despise losing
accept defeat
move on
practice
get better
work harder
make sure it's something you love
something you live to do everyday
over and over again
until you find your world transformed
into the very thing
you thought it could be

Remember when?

Remember when having a dollar was a lot of money?
Going to McDonald's was special
Super Big Gulps were actually super big
The Exorcist scared the shit out of you
The Ninja Turtles Movie was the place to be
Mortal Kombat changed videogames
Hammer pants were cool
Mondetta shirts and Guess jeans were high fashion
Saturday morning cartoons
There was one household telephone and you were lucky to have a beep
A sleep over was a big event
Jason Voorhees was bad ass
Freddy Krueger was scary as fuck
Dumb and Dumber was the funniest movie ever made
Alicia Silverstone in Clueless was the first girl you jerked off too
The chicks thought Jonathan Brandis was hot
People used the word "chick"
The possibility of a spanking was a real thing
Smoking a cigarette was rebellious
When you dated a girl all you did was kiss and those are the kisses you never forget
Renting a video was a family event
Nevermind was released
Live and Unplugged in New York
The Death of Kurt Cobain
Jumping on trampolines was the goal of the summer
The first time you heard "The World is a Vampire..."
Drinking coffee and smoking cigarettes in a restaurant was allowed
When your dreams were still possible
Your life was as free as it was ever gonna be
and the future was something that happened to other people
Me too!
Welcome to reality

amateur cumshot compilation

Go onto a free porn site
Search for amateur cumshot compilation
It'll bring up a bunch
Select anyone to watch
It's hilarious
It usually starts off with an enthusiastic girl
mouth wide open
anxiously waiting
The first shot comes
A look of horror sets in
Her face tenses
Some of them back away as if getting tasered
Others take it in the eye
Sometimes it ends up in their hair or mouth
Hell it probably hits the ceiling
You'd think these guys could aim a little better
Cum in every direction
It's as if the cock is a helicopter blade
The funniest part is the expression on the girl's face
A look of anticipation, confusion and regret all at the same time
Why would you let your boyfriend record himself blowing a load on
your face?
We always tell you we won't show anyone
but the minute we break up
we upload the video directly to the Internet
Don't trust us girls
We're degenerates
Always will be
Enjoy

the success of failure

I've succeeded in so many corporate things
I've worked for a bank 12 years
At 21, I was the youngest manager
I'm 32 now and still the youngest manager
I've won many awards for top performance
Make $100K a year
This is the pinnacle for many people
Everybody thinks I'm a big success
In my mind this is absolute failure
Conforming to other peoples perceptions of reality
eventually results in failure
I'm a musician and writer
I've played several shows to small audiences
I've released my first book
I've made no money off either yet
Most would say I've failed in these areas
but in my reality this is the first time I feel like I've accomplished
something
It seems failure has given much more confidence
and joy to my life then anything else
When you do something you're compelled to do
regardless of failure or success
with no result, expectation or end in mind
then you have truly found something worth doing
Enjoy the doing and everything else will come naturally

I'm gonna

I've heard
    so many
      people say
        I'm gonna
          be a..........
            Police Officer
              when I grow up
                or a Teacher
           a Hockey Player
         a Rockstar
      a Venture Capitalist
    an Actor
Not realizing
    being yourself
      is much more
    important then
      being a profession
    Start with yourself
      and watch
        the doors
      open
       up

Impressed?

It doesn't matter
how many
people
how many
doctors
how many
lawyers
How many
friends you impress along the way
The only thing
that matters
is did you
impress yourself
The rest
is just
vanity

The Birth of the Degenerate

I was born
  on the side of the road
            by the Devil
                  and Jesus won't save me so
I kick back and burn the sky
            with my staring eyes
                  and my fingers mashed up in a clench
Bruce Lee appears in my dreams
                  to fight 7 deadly sins
Kobain strums guitar and tunes a harp
                        like a demon underneath God's wing
Bukowski cries on the inside
      turning his pain into the most beautiful shit
Kerouac's road
    yellow bricked as it was
            found the end
                  was nothing that he ever thought
      Ah here I am
            Born again
    Experience
            my only friend
      Welcome
            to my life
                as
                The Degenerate

The Madness of the Crowd

The crowd
like a slow moving blob
devouring everything
in its path
Plants
Trees
Animals
Humans beware
No one is safe
Encourage their prejudice
Inflate their super ego with a fiery speech
Give them confidence
Steer them
like the
tape worm
they are
War and murder
are the delicacies
they eat
Tread carefully
or they'll tread on you
Think like them
or be crushed by them
Now that's what scares me
The Madness of the Crowd

I'd rather be a Degenerate

I'd rather be a Degenerate
        then a normal person
     hiding behind a veneer
          of beautiful lies
People think money brings happiness
      not realizing purpose is far more important
An Inuit person building an igloo
      with his son
    can be just as happy
      as a rich person
        building a mansion for his family
It's a matter of perspective
   Give that Inuit a million dollars
        and he'll use it to build a fire
Give a rich man the tools to build an igloo
      and he'll pay someone else to do it
 Every person is born
       with a degenerate in them
Find it and you'll find the happiness
      sadness
      failure
    success
      and purpose
    that comes
     with
      it

The Insecurity

Getting closer
      and closer
            to the reality of quitting
                  my job to write
Not knowing what my choice will bring
      The insecurity
            of not having
                  a constant pay cheque haunts me
What happens if I'm not good?
               Become a complete failure
Everyone I know laughs at me
      My former respect gone
        What then?
          F
          R
          E
          E
          D
          O
          M

The Gift of Curse

Sometimes in life you think about the ugly things and become
depressed or angered by them
You don't look like Brad Pitt
You're never gonna be a movie star
Women don't flock to you
Money will be something you always struggle for
Not realizing ugliness is a gift as much as beauty is a curse
It forces you to deal with your brutal truth and hone your talent
It could be writing
or guitar
or sports
or medicine
or, or, or
It focuses you
Becomes your inspiration
Look at yourself
What do you hate most?
Your eyes
Lips
Skin colour
Lack of athletic ability
Your fat belly
Less than perfect tits
When people
       describe your looks
            you get a 6 outta 10
  maybe it's your nose
or your penis size
     Your pay cheque
        Your child's judging eyes
Doesn't matter
Whatever ugliness you have
       compels you to go
           in a certain direction
Follow that direction every day

over and over again
Until the only direction left is death
Treat everyday as if
you live one life
you have to repeat
over
and
over
again
forever
Would you do
what you're doing now
or would you change something?
Most people say they have no regrets
Ask
yourself
this
question
"If I had to do it all again, would I do it all the same?"
A life of no regret
is a life unlived
a life unexamined
a lie
and
far
to common
Live a life of failure
fail beautifully
fail poetically
fail romantically
fail frequently
fail miserably
fail violently
fail
fail
fail
Success

death on his mind

A man walks into a house
            with death on his mind
                the grim reaper in his belt
        black steel
    full clip
        9 Millimeter
He calls out
        "Mom are you here?"
        "Ya honey in the computer room"
He walks a happy, calm walk
Much like a good son would
He comes up behind his mom
    sitting in a chair
            typing on a computer
                waiting for her
                    big 40 year old boy
            to give her a hug
            and
            a
            kiss
    Pulls out his gun
        "I love you Mom"
        "I love you too Son"
        *!@#%**BANG***&%#$
A shot to the back of the head
        "What was that?" his father yells
        "Something happened to Mom – get down here"
    The man waits
        as his father rushes down the stairs
Greasy dirty blonde
        thining curly hair
    Hillbilly
        baseball hat
    Bad Wal-Mart clothes
        A pathetic man

with a Pedophile moustache
Sees his father
Points the gun at his face
     "Why are you doing this son"
     "I'm sorry Dad"
     "Why Son, why?"
     "Money"
     and pulls the trigger

Leavemethefuckaloneist

Communist
Fascist
Socialist
Capitalist
I'm none of these
I'm a leavemethefuckaloneist
This is the political ideology all people should follow
If everybody
        just left everybody else
                the fuck alone
                        this world might be
                                a decent place
Instead we have everybody all up in everybody else's business
Russia leave China alone
North Korea leave South Korea alone
Germany leave Greece alone
America leave everybody alone
Canada used to leave people alone but now they bang the drum for America
I'm the Degenerate
        and
        I'm
        A
leavemethefuckaloneist
        so please
        just leave me
           the fuck
             alone!

Politicians are like Sharks

Politicians are like Sharks
In their environment they're the deadliest killer of all
They stalk their prey
Surprise attacks are their delicacy
Voracious appetites
Kill without thought
Feared by the weaker and smaller fish
Whales know better than to fuck with them
Majestic and powerful hunters of life
Teeth tear into you like statutes through law
When they smell blood they know it's feeding time
But pull those killers out of their environment and watch them flop on
the surface
Weak and pathetic
The once deadly predator is now a useless blob of teeth, whiling on
the ground like a defeated beast
A true fall from grace
How easily a once invincible monster can be killed
Death likes the rich as much as it likes the poor
Don't let sharks scare you
You may get bit
You may lose your life
But it's better to die who you are than live what you're not

I, Sisyphus

I'm like Sisyphus
except I know
the boulder
is made of shit
and everytime
I push it
my hands
get dirtier
and dirtier
The boulder
bigger and bigger
stinkier and stinkier
But I get up
and push
that gross
mass anyways
the poems
stink of it
my life stinks
the world stinks
But I keep writing those poems down
Slowly
they smell
a little better
a flower sprouts out of the shit
little by little hope grows
then another flower springs
and the
next thing
you know
the pile of shit
becomes a bed of flowers
life smells sweeter
days become slower
age grows

as your world
blossoms into
the garden
it was always
meant to be

Wastin'

I sigh thinking about it all
Head hurts
Cooking food
So many things bore me
Toronto
The job
The people
The same thing everyday
Lies, lies and more lies
Rationalization
Different city, same problems
Pressure from all sides
Regret not showing up for things
Regret showing up to things
A bad influence with good intentions
Burned out
Looking forward to taking it easy
Tired, very tired
Alone
Not understanding
Getting by
Coughing
Consider doing it again the same way
Not sure why
But content with right now
My path
and everything that comes with it

Sick day

Call in sick to work
Monday morning
Grey overcast sky
Perfect to watch movies in
Have very little food which means I won't be able to avoid humanity
completely
Lay on the couch
It feels much more comfortable on "sick days"
The water's more refreshing
I'm not as angry
Food tastes better
Masturbation has more pop
Naps of perfect little nothings
A glorious experience of the lazy
If only everyday was a sick day this life would be worth living
Anyone who doesn't prefer the sick day over work is either sicker
then they think or have truly found something worth doing
Which bucket do you fall into?

Joy of the world

My goal
is to travel
the world
the saddest
most decrepit parts
Visit the pain
Find the joy
and write it down
Even the
saddest
moments
can be hilarious
A good friend
passes away
Everyone
gets together
to tell stories
about
that friend
   Laughter
      leads
        to
        tears
  tears
   to
  laughter
laughter
  to
tears
  tears
  to
laughter
  laughter
  to
tears

What

is

life

If

not

laughter

and

t

e

a

r

s

?

Waiting in line for death and coffee

Waiting in L
      I
      N
      E
      for death and coffee
Reading Henry Miller
I stop to drink a Black Girls Ass in
Pink jeans
Round and firm like two soft bowling balls smashed together
I search for panty lines
Find a perfect little T
Ohhh....the small pleasures of waitin
A beautiful smile
Tits in a tight tank top floating like two concrete balloons
A girl bending over just far enough to see her g-string
Lu Lu lemon pants
A man getting punched in the face
The sound of an angry customer who has waited too long
Every once
in a while
amazing
or terrible things
happen while waiting in L
               I
               N
               E
               This makes up for all the other times

Sweet Middle Aged Asian Lady

I walk into a bootleg
        DVD store in Chinatown
Spadina Street
        between Dundas and College
            on the East side
      The normally cheery
      middle aged
        Chinese lady
          is sitting on a stool
            lightly
        sobbing
        to
        herself
    "Is everything ok?" I say
    "No it all bad"
"I'm sorry to hear that" and I walk into the back room to look at the
movies and TV series
Poor girl
I'm guessing her business is closing
There's nothing I want to buy but I do anyways
I pick out two TV series and give her thirty dollars
She gives me a couple free Ninja movies saying "I'm sorry" the
whole time
She's apologizing to me
      even though she's the one
        going out of business!
Finally I find some fucking humanity in this world
Even if on a small scale
I give her a hug and tell her to take care
I hope to see her again before she closes
This poem is dedicated to my sweet little
        middle aged
    DVD bootlegger
      with a heart of gold
    Thank you for everything

Beautiful Mouths

I've had so many beautiful mouths
Indian Mouths
Somalian Mouths
Trinidadian Mouths
Goan Mouths
Japanese Mouths
Half Chinese Mouths
Russian Mouths
Sri Lanken Mouths
Korean mouths
Portuguese Mouths
Bahaman Mouths
Taiwanese Mouths
Jamaican Mouths
Ukrainian Mouths
French Mouths
Irish Mouths
Persian Mouths
Australian Mouths
Panamanian Mouths
Brazilian Mouths
Jewish Mouths
Polish Mouths
       With teeth

and gums made out

of slippery love

and saliva

and soft caressing anger

singing like a wet vacuum

to the world of pleasure

through a vessel of flesh

Thank you

Thank you

Thank you

Thank you all

We're all on the road to death

Wake up
New day
Take a step
All heading towards the same destination

Become famous
or not
Work a shitty job
or be a CEO for a bank

Wake up
New day
Take a step
All heading towards the same destination

Cure cancer
Lead the league in scoring
Kill some motherfuckers
Nuke the earth
Save a kitten from a tree
Sell a mortgage or a pack of cigarettes
Doesn't matter

Wake up
New day
Take a step
All heading towards the same destination

Death

The Immorality of Morality

A man kills another man
                     within their society
He goes on trial for murder
Another man steals something
He's charged with theft
But if a government declares war
                     and sends
                        those
                        same
                        men
                         to
                      another
                   country to kill
                    and steal
     They decorate'em with medals of honour
            Strange Fucken World

Secrets of the Streetcar

Most times on the streetcar you don't want someone sitting beside you

Here are some techniques to keep people away

Technique 1
The Fake Sneeze
If someone is trying to decide who to sit beside use the fake sneeze
Several times if necessary
They might stand instead

Technique 2
Always keep Kleenex on you
Nobody wants to sit beside someone constantly blowing their nose

Technique 3
The Cough
Cough
Cough
Cough
Always cough
It'll keep some people away

Technique 4
Eye Contact
Look people right in the eye as they're walking up to you
It creeps them out and they'll keep walking on by

Technique 5
Combine Tricks 1, 2, 3 and/or 4

Caution these tricks only work 10% of the time.
Never underestimate the laziness of the average person
You could be sitting on a seat
twitching
puking and shitting yourself
and some stupid bastard
or dumb bitch will still sit beside you
But when they don't
Heaven

Ridiculous Advice

Turn on your world
Turn off your TV

Bad Ass

There's a man from Sudbury
a mining man
who went digging for hell
but only found more dirt
With his trusty dog Bill
He can be found at Sugar Lake
playin his guitar
singing songs
from his hero's
Johnny Cash and Neil Young
He's a man that loves trains
Fred Eaglesmith
and the Canadian Way
A true outlaw of his generation
Ramblin down
the highways of time
searching for the next gig
only to find his garage
a cold beer
a smoke
and an old radio
Don't ask him what he thinks about God
cuz he doesn't
Listen for
the echo's
of a man
that can't sing
the blues
no more
who's been Rockin for 52 years
a bad ass like no other
Here's
to
Brian B

The Err of Humanity

They say to be human
is to err

Partially right

I say
to be human
is to destroy
and
create

Creation
through
Destruction

Deconstruct
your past

So you can
create
your
future

The future **is** your past

The Lugee

A woman on the streetcar in front of me
coughs a vile flem filled cough
Hah...cah...hock....hhhuuuucckkk
She looks like a hunchback Grimace
I sense her Lugee building
Gaining strength with each cough
Hak...haochke...haw...ka..ca
Ghoulish
She stands up
Turns around
Walks toward the back of the train and me
Her throat moves
She swallows it
Violation crawls over me like an unwanted finger in the ass
Why do I subject myself to this sick torture?
Everyday a new level of disgust
The man behind me sneezes on my neck
Images of violence flash in my brain
Rage comforts my heart
I turn around
Stare at the man
A dull young effeminate Asian man
Pull out a tissue
Wipe his humanity off my neck
Staring at him the whole time
A very normal stare
A kind serial killer stare
Understanding the situation
He calmly gets up
Walks to the doors and gets off
Now onto my 8 hour shift at the bank
Ain't life swell

Regina Bartendress

Hangin out at a bar in Regina, Saskatchewan with a couple buddies
drinkin half price wine and beers
The Bartendress draws us to the bar with the come hither of her
finger
Awkwardly sexy brunette
Outgoing and funny
Jokes with everyone
Telling us to buy food and more drinks
A good employee really
Seems to enjoy her job which I'm sure she doesn't
Just putting on the happy face to prevent people from askin "What's
wrong?"
I hit the patio for a smoke
Sit at a table by myself
Shortly after she sits down beside me and lights a cigarette
I put my arm around her
and tell her "My friends say you like fat guys"
She laughs "Ya"
"Am I fat enough for you?"
"You're cute" she says
I smile on the inside like I won a fight on the playground
She goes back to work
I finish and head in
We keep drinkin
I tell her she has a nice ass
Reach over the bar and grab it
She says "My boss is here I could get in trouble" and gives me a look
that makes my piece cock-a-doodle-doo
She comes around from the bar to talk to us and stands beside me
I rub her ass
She flexes it
It's firm like a hard flesh pillow
No slap
No anger
Just a purring girl

I go out for another cigarette
She walks by the window
I motion with my hand to come join me
She shakes her head and tells me with her eyes to come with her
We go to a private patio where the employees smoke
I sit beside her
Tell her I like her
I try kissing her but she won't let me
She gives up her neck and I suck on it gently
I go for the mouth
She's receptive but no tongue
I look at her breasts not understanding why I didn't notice them
before
I whisper in her ear
"Give me some tongue baby"
She does
I reach down the top of her shirt
underneath her bra and rub her breast
Round, beautiful, soft, heaven
I pull it out slowly
Her nipple is perfect
small
appetizing
I understand a babies urge to suck
and I do
We're interrupted by a co-worker
A Gorilla of a Man
I stand up to leave
My cock raging
"Jesus Christ man I can see your boner though you're shorts"
"Sorry" I say like a guilty child and run inside to meet my friends
A couple hours later she tells me she's going to the washroom
"The second door on the right, meet me in two minutes"
I knock
She let's me in
Immediately she starts grabbing my unit
Kisses me hard

Drops to her knees
Undoes my pants
Rips it out and starts sucking
I enjoy it for a few seconds
Pull her up
Flip her over
Pull her pants down and say "You want it"
"Yaa"
I stick it in 7 or 8 times
Hard Angry Thrusts
Pull her hair
Push her head up against the wall above the toilet
Ramming her the whole time
"I…I…uhhh..I gotta gooo…umm…uhhh…back to..ah..work" she says
Pulls her pants up
Kisses me and leaves
I finish myself off faster then you can switch on a light
It could be worse
I could be at the bar drinking with my friends dreaming of a moment
like this
Instead I get the real thing
Fuck it's good to be me

My Generation

My Generation is in a recession
Naw a spiritual depression
We're sick and tired of all these corporations
Stealing our nations
With their documentation
Secret associations
Handshakes and nudges
Bought and paid for judges
Prime Ministers
Presidents
Elected Representatives
You don't think they conspire
Prove I'm a liar
Cuz I'm on a mission
To change your disposition
But first things first

WAKE UP MY GENERATION

My Generation better not get it twisted
No you're not the victim
But an active participant
In a system
Old as the ages
Babylon would praise us
As its natural successor
Born to replace her
But I'm here to warn ya
Like Jonah before me
Those who can listen
Change your disposition
But first things first

WAKE UP MY GENERATION

Acknowledgements:

Thanks to my Pa Pa for raising my 2 brothers, my sister and I. Without him I wouldn't be the degenerate I am today.

Contact Information

Matt Ross
kingofthedregs@live.com
Like me at www.facebook.com/thedegenerate

www.ingramcontent.com/pod-product-compliance
Lightning Source LLC
Chambersburg PA
CBHW071724110426
42740CB00057B/2811